Fact Finders®

FAIRGROUND RIDES

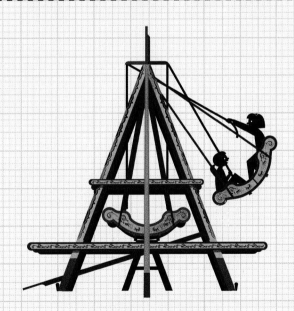

SALLY SPRAY
WITH ARTWORK BY MARK RUFFLE

CAPSTONE PRESS
a capstone imprint

Fact Finders Books are published by Capstone Press,
1710 Roe Crest Drive, North Mankato, Minnesota 56003
www.mycapstone.com

Library of Congress Cataloging-in-Publication Data
Library of Congress Cataloging-in-Publication data is available on the Library of Congress website.

978-1-5435-1335-6 (library binding)
978-1-5435-1341-7 (paperback)

Editorial Credits

Series editor: Paul Rockett
Series design and illustration: Mark Ruffle
www.rufflebrothers.com
Consultant:
Andrew Woodward BEng (Hons) CEng MICE FCIArb

Photo Credits

Casiohabib/Shutterstock: 13b. Kobby Dagan/Shutterstock: 29cl. EPA/Alamy: 24b. Funtime Group:
23t, 23b. Keasbury Gordon Photograph Archive/Alamy: 4t. Rene Kohut/Shutterstock: 29cr. Kazuhi-
ro Nogi/AFP/Getty Images: 26c. Barry Norman Collection/Mary Evans PL: 11c. Pbombaert/Shut-
terstock: 17b. Photogolfer/Shutterstock: 29c. Mark Ruffle: 7. Nik Taylor/Alamy: 21t. Anthony Aneese
Totah Jr/Dreamstime: 29tr. Buddhika Weerasinghe/Getty Images: 28cr. WENN Ltd./Alamy: 28c.
Wentworth Collection/Mary Evans PL: 19t. Wikimedia Commons: 9b, 15b, 28t.

First published in Great Britain in 2017
by The Watts Publishing Group
Copyright © The Watts Publishing Group, 2017

Printed and bound in China.
010755S18

TABLE OF CONTENTS

ALL THE FUN OF THE FAIR!

Fairgrounds are places for thrills and scares on daredevil rides. Over the years, rides have become more and more terrifying as designers and **engineers** seek to create the ultimate experience for thrill seekers.

HOW DID FAIRS BEGIN?

Fairs started when people got together to buy and sell items, find work, or celebrate festivals. One of the earliest was the Stagshaw Bank Fair in Northumberland, England, which started as a gathering for selling animals around 1293. By the 1850s, fairs had games, exhibits, and rides to entertain the crowds.

Carousels and rides have been part of the St. Giles Fair in Oxford, England, for more than 150 years.

RIDES of the WORLD

Wooden roller coaster
The fastest wooden roller coaster with the highest drop (180 feet) is Goliath at Six Flags Great America, in Gurnee, Illinois.

4th dimension (4D) roller coaster
*The first **4D roller coaster** was X. It opened in 2002 at Six Flags Magic Mountain in California. Some changes were made in 2008, and it is now called X2.*

Carousel
The world's largest indoor carousel is at House on the Rock in Spring Green, Wisconsin. It has 269 carousel animals and 20,000 lights.

Dating back to 1780, the world's oldest carousel is in Wilhelmsbad Park, Hanau, Germany.

Bumper cars
One of the most unusual places for a bumper-car ride is on board the cruise ship Quantum of the Seas.

4

FAIR POWER

Basic rides like swingboats, 'over the top' wheels, and carousels developed over time into the exciting rides we know today. Early rides were powered by hand, sometimes by children in return for a free go! Larger rides, like carousels, were horse powered.

From the 1860s, steam power took over and **traction engines** were used to move the rides. Later, these amazing machines were replaced by electricity.

Fairgrounds have adapted existing machines that used basic engineering like wheels, cogs, and chains. Many rides share the same principles of **forces** and motion, but they change the experience by adding extra speed, height, turns, or total darkness for even bigger shocks and scares. So, sit down, hold on tight, and enjoy the ride!

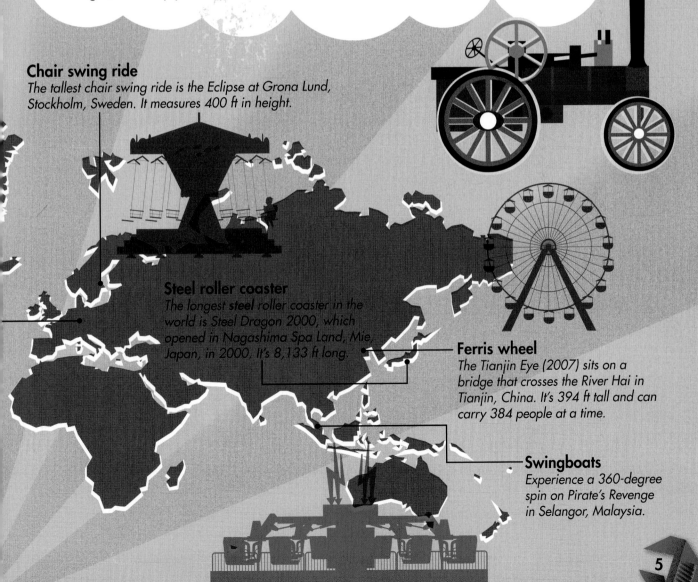

Chair swing ride
The tallest chair swing ride is the Eclipse at Grona Lund, Stockholm, Sweden. It measures 400 ft in height.

Steel roller coaster
The longest steel roller coaster in the world is Steel Dragon 2000, which opened in Nagashima Spa Land, Mie, Japan, in 2000. It's 8,133 ft long.

Ferris wheel
The Tianjin Eye (2007) sits on a bridge that crosses the River Hai in Tianjin, China. It's 394 ft tall and can carry 384 people at a time.

Swingboats
Experience a 360-degree spin on Pirate's Revenge in Selangor, Malaysia.

SWINGBOATS

One of the very first rides to become popular at traveling fairs was the swingboat. The swingboat's backward and forward swinging motion formed the basis of future fairground attractions known as **pendulum** rides.

BUILDING BRIEF

Build a hand-powered ride based on a swinging or pendulum motion.

Inventor: Swingboats have been around since the early 1800s; the inventor is unknown.

Key location: The Skylark at the Beamish Open-Air Museum in England is one of the oldest swingboats in the world. It dates back to the 1830s.

Axle attached to the top of the **A-frame**

Rope

Rope

Boat, also called a gondola

Swingboats in action

PULLING POWER

Swingboats need muscle power to get them started. Riders pull on hanging ropes to make the boat swing. As one rider pulls down on his or her rope, the nose of the boat rises. As the boat swings back in an arc, the opposite rider pulls on his or her rope, and the swingboat goes higher in the opposite direction.

GIANT PENDULUM

A swingboat acts like a giant pendulum, swinging in a fixed path under its own weight. It needs power to make it move upward for the first swing, then **gravity** pulls the boat down. A force called **inertia** keeps it moving, pushing the swingboat back into the air. This process works again and again to make the boat swing back and forth. Riders can keep pulling on the ropes to pull the boat into the air and maintain the **momentum** of this swinging sensation!

NEWTON'S FIRST LAW OF MOTION

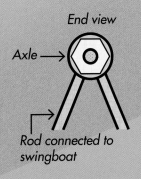

End view

Axle →

Rod connected to swingboat

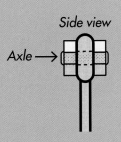

Side view

Axle →

The constant swinging motion of a swingboat is an example of Newton's first **law of motion**, which says that an object that is still will stay still unless it is moved, and an object that is moving will stay moving unless something stops it.

When the riders stop pulling on the ropes, **friction** starts to slow down the boat. Friction occurs as the surfaces of the axle and the rods rub against each other. Friction also occurs from air resistance as the boat pushes through the air. Eventually friction brings the boat to a halt.

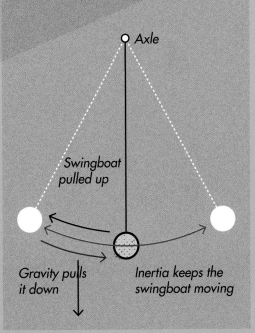

Axle

Swingboat pulled up

Gravity pulls it down

Inertia keeps the swingboat moving

MAUCH CHUNK SWITCHBACK RAILWAY

The Mauch Chunk Switchback Railway in Pennsylvania was the first roller coaster in the United States. But it wasn't designed to be a fun ride. When it was built in 1827, it was designed to transport coal.

BECOMING A RIDE

The railway began taking passengers in 1829. At first, the uphill journey was powered by mules pulling the carriage along a single-track railroad. This took four hours, whereas gravity powered the speedy half-hour ride downhill. Passengers found the journey thrilling and flocked to ride on it. For over 50 years beginning in 1872, it was run entirely for fun and carried more than 35,000 passengers a year.

BUILDING BRIEF

Build a railroad to move coal between Mauch Chunk and Summit Hill.

Engineer: Josiah White

Location: Pennsylvania, USA

*Rails work by guiding the train or carriage over a set route. The rails provide a low-friction track, which transfers some of the weight of the train to the ground through the **sleepers** and loose **ballast** surround. The rails are fixed to the sleepers but are not fixed to the ballast, so as the train moves over the rails, its weight is transferred to the ground.*

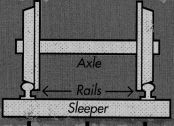

Axle

Rails

Sleeper

Loose ballast →

Ground

ANTI-ROLLBACK DEVICE

In 1846, the mules were retired and the carriages were pulled uphill by a **winch** and cable. A new **ratchet** safety feature was also fitted to the underside of the carriages. This was the first kind of anti-rollback device. A device called a pawl hangs from the underside of the car and catches on a ratchet strip on the track. This simple **mechanism** stops the cars from rolling downhill if the cable breaks. The ratchet and pawl make a loud, clickety-clack sound as they knock together. The device is still used on roller coasters today, and coaster enthusiasts love the tension this builds on the steep uphill climb.

Pawl →

Ratchet

The Switchback Railway at Coney Island opened in 1884. It was the first American roller coaster built as a ride, and it featured two parallel hilly tracks. Riders sat on a seat similar to a park bench and traveled sideways down the track. They sped along one track to the end, got off, and then the park bench and riders were switched onto the other track to whoosh back to the beginning.

CAROUSEL

Carousels, also known as merry-go-rounds or flying horses, are **iconic** fairground rides. The first carousels were simple wooden structures with horses that didn't move. These early carousels were powered by horses or people. But it was the adoption of steam power in the mid-1800s that really got carousels galloping!

BUILDING BRIEF

Create a carousel that is not powered by horses or people, and add a galloping motion.

Inventors: Thomas Bradshaw invented the steam-powered carousel in 1861; Frederick Savage's galloping mechanism first appeared in 1870.

Location: Norfolk, England

Around 140 pounds of coal were needed to power the carousel's steam engine for one day of rides.

STEAM GALLOPERS

In 1861 Thomas Bradshaw built the first set of steam-powered carousel horses. He called this ride a galloper. The steam engine turns a drive shaft that has a cog at the end of it. This cog turns an angled bevel **gear** that is fixed to an upright pole. This in turn moves a ring gear in the **canopy** and the carousel spins around.

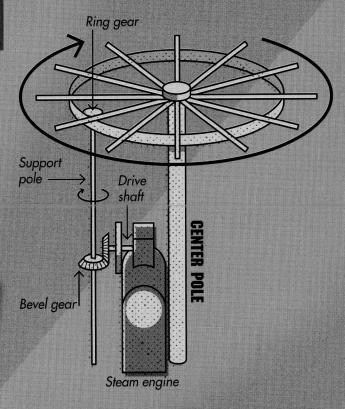

Ring gear

Support pole →

Drive shaft

CENTER POLE

Bevel gear

Steam engine

A steam-driven galloper in London, 1903

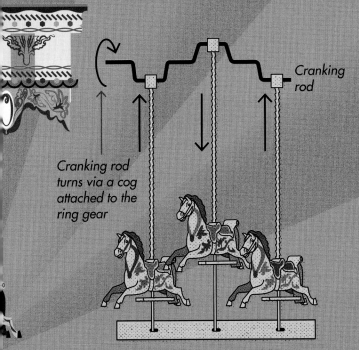

Cranking rod

Cranking rod turns via a cog attached to the ring gear

GEARS AND CRANKS

Later in 1870, Frederick Savage added a gear and offset crank mechanism to his steam-powered horses, making them rise and fall at different times during the ride. Savage connected each horse to a **cranking rod** in the canopy via a pole. Savage made the cranking rods wiggly, not straight, so each horse connected to them hung at a different height.

As the ride rotates, so does the cranking rod. This causes the horses to be lifted and lowered at different times as if they are galloping. The pole that each horse is attached to goes through a hole in the floor's platform. This hole allows the poles to move forward a little as the ride goes faster.

CHAIR SWING RIDE

Chair swing rides, also known as Chair-O-Planes or wave swingers, developed from carousels. One of the first steam-driven rides was built by John Inshaw in 1888. On these types of rides, the seats are not restrained at the bottom and the passengers are lifted into the air on swing seats, flying outward as the central column of the ride spins faster and faster.

BUILDING BRIEF

Use the spinning steam-driven technology of the carousel to create a new and wilder ride.

Inventor: John Inshaw

Key locations:
Chair-O-Plane (1888), Birmingham, England

SkyScreamer (2011),
Six Flags, New Jersey, USA

FORCES

The central frame of the swing ride rotates at speeds up to 43 miles per hour (mph). In reaction to the spinning force, the hanging seats fly out to the side. This movement is caused by the balancing of two opposing forces—centrifugal and centripetal force.

CENTRIFUGAL FORCE pushes outward, moving the seats away from the center of the ride.

CENTRIPETAL FORCE pushes the seats back in toward the center. The opposition of these two forces creates tension in the chairs' chains, making the chairs rise to an almost **horizontal** level and giving the riders an amazing flying sensation.

Centrifugal force

Centripetal force

Center of the ride

The faster the ride rotates, the farther the seats swing out.

SKYSCREAMER

In 2011, the SkyScreamer (pictured), an extreme version of a swing ride, opened at Six Flags in New Jersey. The SkyScreamer is the tallest in the world, lifting riders over 240 ft into the air and rotating them at 40 mph. The tower is made up of six upright struts that are joined together by a pattern of diagonal supports. The crisscross design makes it strong and allows the wind to whistle through the structure, keeping it from swaying and bending out of shape.

SIX FLA

FERRIS WHEEL

The first Ferris wheel was built as a giant engineering spectacle for visitors to the World's Columbian Exposition in Chicago, Illinois, in 1893. The upright 264-foot-tall wheel had room for 2,160 passengers at a time!

BUILDING BRIEF

Design a ride built of steel that will astound and delight visitors to the World's Columbian Exposition, held to celebrate the 400th anniversary of Columbus landing in America.

Inventor: George Washington Gale Ferris Jr.

Key location: Chicago, Illinois, USA

UPWARD AND DOWNWARD

Ferris's super-strong steel structure consisted of a large wheel rotating on a central axis held by two towers. The ride upward was powered by a steam engine driving the turns with the help of gears, like a giant carousel turned on its side. The ride downward was helped by the pull of gravity and kept under control by the gear mechanism.

Even today, the passenger cars hang off axles at the edge of the wheel. They swing as the ride moves, but gravity keeps them hanging downward and the riders safely in their seats.

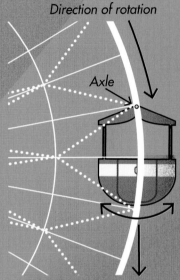

Direction of rotation

Axle

Pull of gravity

THE POWER OF THE TRIANGLE

The Ferris wheel is held in place by a large steel triangular frame. The spokes of the wheel fan outward in a triangular shape. Ferris knew through designing and building bridges that long spans of wood or metal could be strengthened by adding crisscross supports that make triangular shapes. The triangle is the strongest shape to use because forces move evenly throughout the three sides and corners. As a result, the triangle is more successful at resisting **stress** than other shapes.

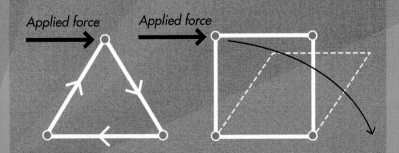

Applied force *Applied force*

When the wheel was unveiled, George W. Ferris said he had gotten the wheels out of his head and made them a living reality.

BUMPER CARS

Electric bumper cars are one of the most popular fairground rides of all time. Also known as dodgems, these small cars with their big, rubber bumpers allow anyone—no matter how young or how old—to drive, ram, bump, and crash into each other.

BUILDING BRIEF

Build a ride that is controlled by the rider—a car that can be driven, raced, and bumped all around the track.

Inventors: Max and Harold Stoehrer

Key location: Methuen, Massachusetts, USA

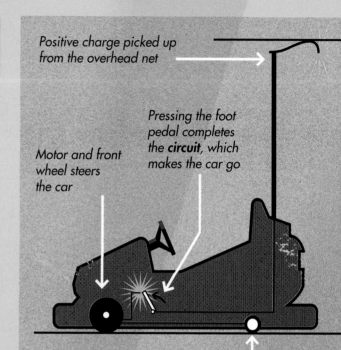

Positive charge picked up from the overhead net

Pressing the foot pedal completes the **circuit**, which makes the car go

Motor and front wheel steers the car

Negative charge picked up from the floor

BUMPER CAR CIRCUIT

One of the major innovations that changed fairground rides was the introduction of electricity. The first bumper cars worked by completing a simple electrical circuit. The power supply ran through an overhead net and traveled down to the car through a metal pole. The cars had three wheels—two rubber ones at the back and a metal one in the front to conduct electricity. The track surface was also conductive. When the bumper car pedal was pressed, the electrical circuit was complete. The motor rotated the wheels via a belt and the car jumped into action.

BUMPING MOTION

When bumper cars ram into each other, we have a perfect example of Newton's third law of motion. This states that for every action there is an equal and opposite reaction.

As the cars collide, the force with which they are moving and the **mass** they contain gets distributed around the rubber bumper. This also makes the riders jolt as the energy transfers between the cars. Each collision is different because of the speed, the direction the cars travel, and the weight of the riders.

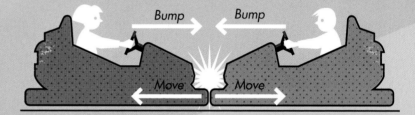

Modern bumper cars are powered by metal strips on the floor, which connect to brushes under the cars.

BIG DIPPER

People love to be scared and what better way to be terrified than to speed around a rickety wooden track in a tiny car at great speed? The Big Dipper at Blackpool Pleasure Beach, which opened in 1923, does just that. It was the first roller coaster in the UK that included a big drop and a complete circuit. The Big Dipper is still thrilling riders today.

BUILDING BRIEF

Design a spectacular ride for Blackpool Pleasure Beach, a British theme park.

Inventor: John A. Miller, 1923

Location: Blackpool, UK

Lift-hill mechanism

Chain dogs

LIFT-HILL MECHANISM

The Big Dipper starts with a long, steep climb followed by a massive drop. The climb is supported by the lift-hill mechanism, which was invented in 1885, by Phillip Hinkle. This has a looped chain running around two wheels at the top and bottom of the upward track. The chain is exposed to the underside of the car as it moves along the rails. Chain dogs, which are big hooks hanging down from the car, catch onto the chain. This drags the car upward. When the chain dog is released at the top of the hill, gravity takes over, and the car plunges down the track.

The Big Dipper at Blackpool Pleasure Beach, 1930s

In 1919 John A. Miller also invented an anti-rollback device called the upstop wheel. If the chain breaks on the uphill climb, this third wheel under the rails keeps the cars from rolling back down the track.

POTENTIAL AND KINETIC ENERGY

The Big Dipper is an "out and back" roller coaster, meaning that it runs in a complete circuit. After the initial big climb and spectacular fall, the rest of the ride is tamer because the car is powered by the potential and **kinetic energy** produced on that first big opening climb and drop.

As the car goes uphill, it gathers **potential energy**, and at the top of the climb, it stops. At this point, because of the height, it has reached the point of maximum potential energy. The potential energy changes into kinetic energy to power the car for the rest of the ride. The balance of potential and kinetic energy was carefully considered by engineers who designed the Big Dipper so the car could complete its run.

Wooden roller coasters are often built from pine or Douglas fir trees, which grow strong and straight. ➔

● Potential energy

● Maximum potential energy

Kinetic energy

ORBITER

With its use of **hydraulics**, the Orbiter was a new and **innovative** ride when it launched in 1976. It's a fast-paced spinning ride that quickly became a favorite for fairground thrill seekers.

BUILDING BRIEF

Use hydraulics to create a fairground ride that is fast, exciting, and totally new!

Inventors: Richard Woolls

Key location: First appeared in Margate, England

MOVEMENTS

The Orbiter moves in three ways: the cars move around in a circle; the cars move up and down as the main arms rise and fall on a 90-degree angle; the cars at the end of the arm spin. These three movements create a wildly exciting ride pattern. The use of hydraulics makes the ride exceptionally quiet, but an explosion of lights and music make up for the lack of mechanical noise.

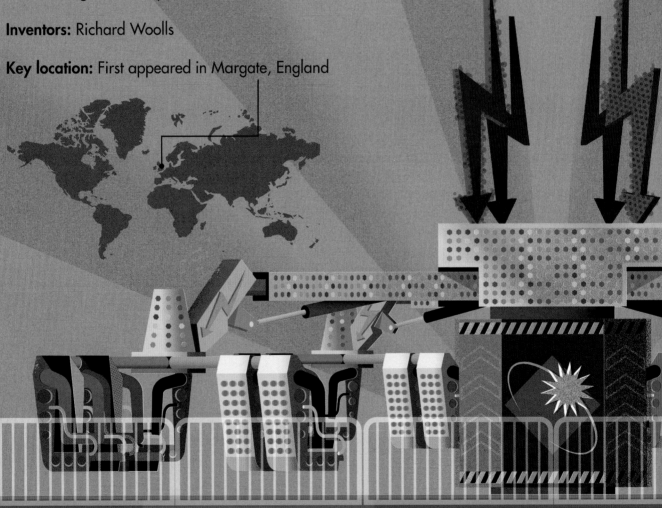

HOW DO HYDRAULICS WORK?

Hydraulics work by placing a force onto one point, which then moves another point. The force is transferred through a liquid that cannot be compressed, in this case oil. The oil presses against the **pistons**, and the pistons move the arms of the Orbiter.

The hydraulic system has to be closed with enough power in the engine and enough liquid in the system to move the arms on the Orbiter upward. When the ride is finished, an opposite pressure has to be applied to the arm system to make it come back down to the ground.

The center part of the ride lifts off the ground with more hydraulics. Once it has lifted the riders off the ground, it starts to rotate. The central column rotates at 20 revolutions per minute (rpm) and the arms at 30 rpm, resulting in a fast-moving whirlwind of a ride!

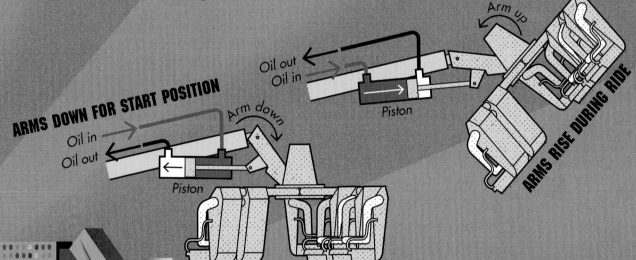

ARMS DOWN FOR START POSITION

Oil in
Oil out
Arm down
Piston

Oil out
Oil in
Arm up
Piston

ARMS RISE DURING RIDE

HYDRAULIC REVOLUTION

Since the Orbiter, hydraulic engineering has become a common feature in fairground rides. It is used in the breaking and launching systems on roller coasters and to lower and secure the safety restraints that hold passengers in their seats.

SLINGSHOT

Unveiled in 2004, the Slingshot is like a huge **catapult**. It has a car holding two passengers that is connected to twin towers by steel cables. The car is anchored at ground level, and when released, it shoots the car up into the sky. For riders, the sensation is like that of an arrow being fired from a bow. It's like a bungee jump in reverse!

SPRING TIME

Some catapult rides have elastic bungee ropes that fling the passenger carriage into the air. But the Slingshot uses an advanced system of **springs** and **pulleys** to power the car. When the seat is secured to the ground, the coiled springs are stretched out. Then, when the slingshot car is released, the springs shoot back into their coiled shape, thrusting the car high into the air.

BUILDING BRIEF

Construct a ride based on the idea of a slingshot, which propels the riders high into the air.

Manufacturer: Funtime, Bundall, Australia

Key location: Bundall, Australia

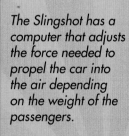

The Slingshot has a computer that adjusts the force needed to propel the car into the air depending on the weight of the passengers.

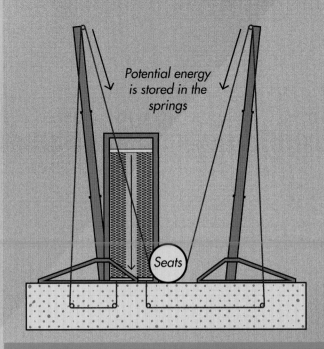

Potential energy is stored in the springs

The towers of the Slingshot are 200 ft tall.

ENERGY TRANSFER

Before the ride starts, the tension in the cable is storing potential energy. Once the catapult is released and the car springs upward, it becomes kinetic energy, the energy of motion. Potential energy is created by the height the car continues to climb to, and kinetic energy is released on the downward path.

The Slingshot uses 720 springs to fire people up, up, and away!

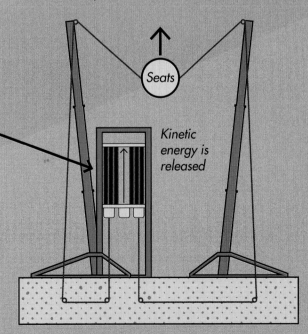

Kinetic energy is released

KINGDA KA AND ZUMANJARO

If one fairground ride seems a bit dull, how about two rides joined together? Kingda Ka runs along twisting tubular steel tracks that allow it to loop and corkscrew through 360 degrees. Zumanjaro is a drop ride that sits on the curving loop of the Kingda Ka. Together, they add up to two truly terrifying rides.

BUILDING BRIEF

Build a super-fast and tall roller coaster, then add to the feeling of danger by linking it to a terrifying drop ride.

Designer: Kingda Ka: Werner Stengel; Zumanjaro: Michael Reitz

Manufacturer: Intamin

Map location: Jackson, New Jersey, USA

The tubular steel tracks allow for a 360-degree twisting corkscrew turn.

STATION

Cars

KINGDA KA

At 456 ft, Kingda Ka is the tallest roller coaster in the world. It's a simple loop-coaster, with lots of corkscrew twists. The car is propelled along the track at great speed by a hydraulic launch system. The car is hooked onto an extended cable, which is connected to a winch drum powered by hydraulic motors. The motor spins the winch drum, winding in the cable at high speed. This action pulls the cable and attached car along the track and then shoots the car off to speed over the gigantic loop before dropping straight down on its way back to the station.

It takes the car only 3.5 seconds to reach 128 mph, and the whole ride is over in just 28 seconds.

ZUMANJARO

Its official name is Zumanjaro: Drop of Doom. And as the name suggests, this is a drop ride. It winches three horizontal cars holding 24 people up the 415-foot frame using a cable. The tension builds as the cars climb slowly to the top, halting for a few seconds, then the car plummets down to earth at 90 mph!

Zumanjaro uses an **electromagnetic** brake system. This works by having a copper **conductor** attached to the car and a **magnetic field** at the bottom of the drop. When the conductor on the car reaches the magnet, it creates its own magnetic field, and when one magnetic field moves over another, they react by producing an opposing force. In this case, it is an upward force at the bottom that slows down the car, stopping the freefall.

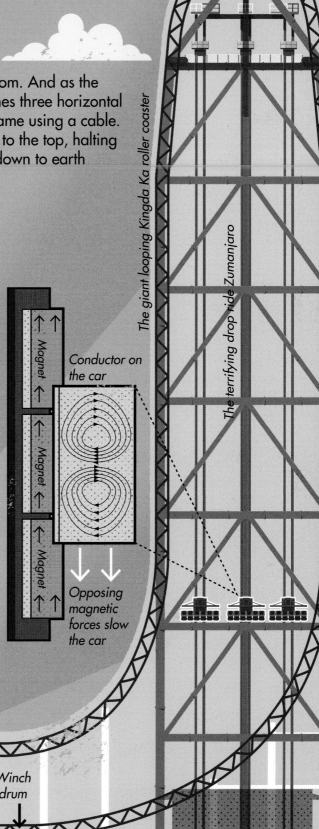

The giant looping Kingda Ka roller coaster

The terrifying drop ride Zumanjaro

Magnet

Magnet

Magnet

Conductor on the car

Opposing magnetic forces slow the car

FREEFALL SENSATIONS

Both these rides play with your senses as they go into freefall. The acceleration of the ride pushing you back in your seat is equal to the force of gravity pulling you forward out of your seat, which makes you feel momentarily weightless.

Cable

Winch drum

EEJANAIKA

Opened in 2006, Eejanaika is a roller coaster with a twist. The riders sit in seats that extend over either side of the track to give the feeling of hanging in the air. As the car speeds and turns, riders experience extra spins as the seats turn independently. This is what makes the Eejanaika a 4th dimension roller coaster.

THE NEXT DIMENSION

The Eejanaika features only three upside-down turns, known as inversions, but with the added spin of the seats, riders are turned a tummy-twisting 14 times during the ride. The seats are rotated on a horizontal axis that sticks out **perpendicular** to the track. Those tracks are the key to the extra spins.

The ride has two sets of tracks that run alongside each other—one set for the cars to run on, the other set to control the seat turns. In certain places, the tracks run closer together, which engages a simple rack-and-pinion system that sends the seats spinning.

Riders in a spin on Eejanaika

BUILDING BRIEF

Put a new spin on roller coaster technology to give riders a whirl of a time.

Designer: S&S Arrow

Key location: Fuji-Q Highland, Yamanashi, Japan

LIFT
The car climbs up the lift toward the first terrifying drop.

STATION

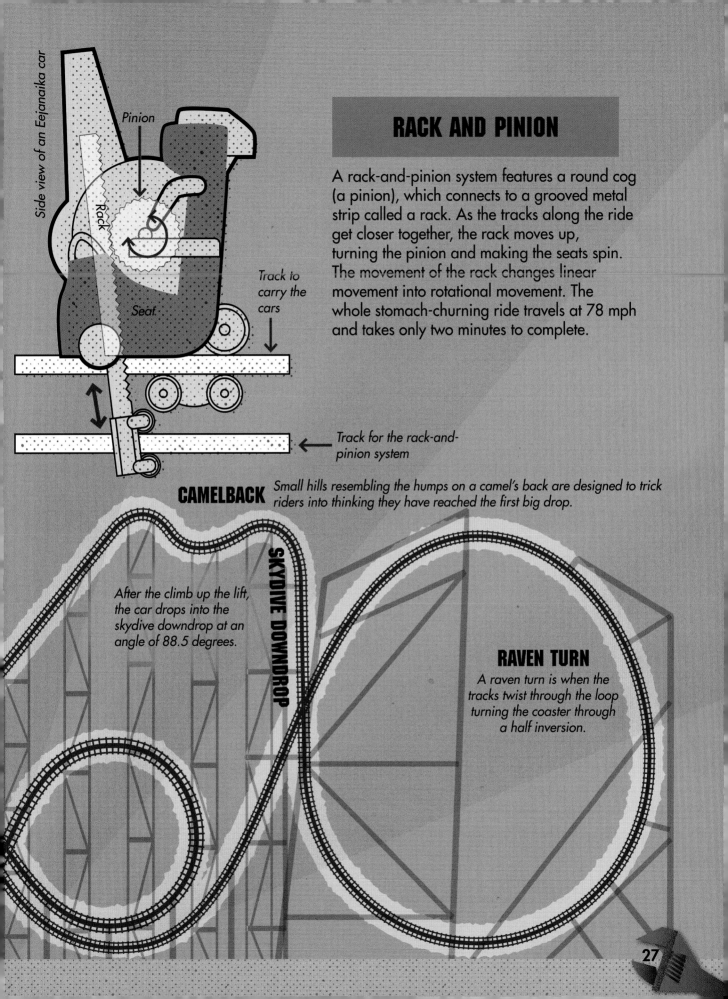

Side view of an Eejanaika car

Pinion

Rack

Seat

Track to carry the cars

Track for the rack-and-pinion system

RACK AND PINION

A rack-and-pinion system features a round cog (a pinion), which connects to a grooved metal strip called a rack. As the tracks along the ride get closer together, the rack moves up, turning the pinion and making the seats spin. The movement of the rack changes linear movement into rotational movement. The whole stomach-churning ride travels at 78 mph and takes only two minutes to complete.

CAMELBACK *Small hills resembling the humps on a camel's back are designed to trick riders into thinking they have reached the first big drop.*

SKYDIVE DOWNDROP

After the climb up the lift, the car drops into the skydive downdrop at an angle of 88.5 degrees.

RAVEN TURN

A raven turn is when the tracks twist through the loop turning the coaster through a half inversion.

FASCINATING FACTS

Fairground rides are constantly changing as engineers seek different ways to move the rider or the carriage around.

One of the earliest roller coaster rides was Les Montagnes Russes à Belleville, which appeared in France in 1817. It featured a heart-shaped design with two cars loading at the top of the track and then racing downhill in opposite directions. Each car gathered enough momentum on the way down to power the cars back up the slope to meet again at the top.

Shweeb in New Zealand is a pedal-powered eco ride. Schweeb has one-person pods attached to an overhead rail. Riders climb in, lie down, and pedal as fast as they can around the track. The pods can reach speeds up to 31 mph.

Skycycle in Japan is another pedal-powered eco ride. It is much slower than Shweeb but no less scary, as twin-pedaled bikes travel along the track high above the ground.

The first helter skelter was seen at a fair in Hull, England, in 1905. The pull of gravity and a smooth slide transport riders around and around in a spiral down to the bottom of a tower.

LAS VEGAS

The Stratosphere hotel in Las Vegas, Nevada, has four terrifying rides at the top of its 1,149-foot tower.

Thrill seekers bungee jump 855 ft from the Sky Jump at the Stratosphere hotel.

The X-Scream sends riders over the edge of the tower, where the track seesaws to make them think they'll fall 866 ft to the ground.

On Insanity, a gigantic arm extends 64 feet beyond the edge of the tower, spinning and tilting riders to give them a stomach-churning view of Las Vegas.

The Big Shot is a drop ride that uses **pneumatic** motors to shoot riders up to a height of 1,081 ft above ground level . . . and back down to the tower again.

READ MORE

Black, Vanessa. *Kingda Ka Roller Coaster*. Engineering Marvels. Minneapolis, Minn.: Jump!, Inc., 2017.

Glatzer, Jenna. *George Ferris' Grand Idea: The Ferris Wheel*. The Story Behind the Name. North Mankato, Minn.: Capstone Press, 2016.

Loh-Hagan, Virginia. *Roller Coasters*. 21st Century Junior Library: Extraordinary Engineering. Ann Arbor, Mich.: Cherry Lake Publishing, 2017.

Spilsbury, Louise. *Ride that Rollercoaster!: Forces in an Amusement Park*. Feel the Force. Chicago, Ill.: Heinemann Raintree, 2016.

INTERNET SITES

FactHound offers a safe, fun way to find Internet sites related to this book. All of the sites on FactHound have been researched by our staff.

Here's all you do:

Visit www.facthound.com

Type in this code: 9781543513356

Check out projects, games and lots more at
www.capstonekids.com